Santa Barbara

Santa Barbara Mission

A 2-Day Itinerary

By Clare Auchterlonie

Table of Contents

Introduction

Just two hours north of Los Angeles, beautiful adobe buildings topped with red stucco roofs are nestled against the Santa Ynez Mountains in front of the Pacific Ocean. This little slice of paradise is the American Riviera - Santa Barbara!

Santa Barbara is a great place to escape from the hustle and bustle of city living. There's plenty to see in this small beach town, from world famous art to boutique shopping, alfresco dining, sipping on award-winning wines and beers, just lounging on the beach, or visiting a first class zoo - Santa Barbara has something for everyone.

This trip provides the complete trip experience - how to get there, where to stay, great places to eat, and what to see. This detailed itinerary will guarante that you have fun, save money, and see a wide range of what the area has to offer - not just the popular places, but local favorites as well.

Days of this tour can be swapped around according to your needs:

Day 1 - Explore the history of the American Riviera and discover how this paradise came to be.

Day 2 - Enjoy the best of the area's scenic outdoors, and reward yourself by enjoying the fruits (grapes) of the soil.

Included

- Lots of tips about visiting Santa Barbara

- Where to stay, no matter your budget.

- Suggestions on how to save money on your trip.

- The best lunch and dinner suggestions to suit your wallet.

- Pictures and maps of locations to help guide you around without a smartphone.

- Days of the tour can be easily swapped around for your convenience.

- Tons of activity suggestions if you want to extend your trip.

- Most destinations are suitable for travellers of any age (with alternative suggestions for those that are not).

Day 1

=============

9:00 am -- Breakfast at The Daily Grind

- **Price:** $10.00 (for a single adult)
- **Duration:** 1 hour
- **Address:** 2001 De La Vina Santa Barbara, CA

Picture from The Daily Grind Facebook.

If your hotel does not provide breakfast, then here are some recommendations:

The Daily Grind is a popular place to grab a decent cup of coffee and a bagel. If you're looking for something more substantial, then the breakfast burrito is an excellent choice. The staff is friendly, and they have a nice outdoor patio with off-street parking.

If you're looking for something fancier, walk into **Dawn Patrol** on State Street and build your own hash, or **The Shop Cafe** for an authentic window-serve café experience – the oatmeal and the 'Rollex' breakfast wraps are big hits.

Wherever you get your breakfast on, eat up because you have a big day ahead!

10:00 am -- Drive to Santa Barbara Mission

- **Price:** FREE
- **Duration:** 10 minutes

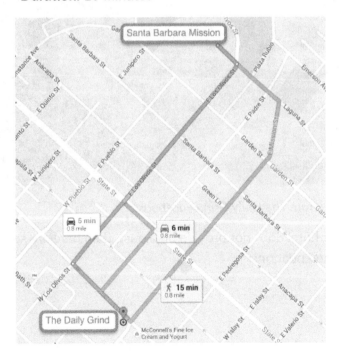

Directions from The Daily Grind: Head southeast on Laguna St toward E Los Olivos St. Turn right onto W Los Olivos Street and then left onto E Mission. A free parking lot is to the left of the **Santa Barbara Mission** and well sign posted - be sure to go in the second entrance (the first is the exit!). If there are a ton of coaches, the parking lot is large and should be plenty of room, however, if you don't want to deal with it, you can park on the street and walk up – just be wary of parking notices.

10:10 am -- Santa Barbara Mission

- **Price:** $8.00 (for a single adult)
- **Duration:** 50 minutes
- **Address:** 2201 Laguna St, Santa Barbara, CA 93101

Santa Barbara Mission was founded in 1786 by Spanish Franciscans - it was the tenth of twenty-one missions they founded in California. Although an earthquake destroyed the original building in 1812, it was rebuilt and dedicated in 1820. The Mission is named after **Saint Barbara** a young girl who was supposedly beheaded by her father for choosing to follow Christianity.

Over 200 years later, the mission is still used as the community's religious hub with various significant events taking place throughout the year, including a live nativity scene complete with real sheep and donkeys, and **I Madonnari**, the Italian street painting festival in May where the slabs in front of the mission are painted in wonderful bright chalk drawings.

You can **wander the grounds for free** – be sure to **check out the rose garden** directly in front of the mission. You can take a self-guided tour for $8 or take a guided tour for $12. For times and details (including discounts) **see website**.

11:00 am -- Drive to Santa Barbara Historical Museum

- **Price:** FREE
- **Duration:** 10 minutes

Head southwest on Laguna Street away from the Mission back towards E Los Olivos. Take this for 1.5 miles till you get to E De La Guerra Street, turn right. If you can't find street parking, park in one of the city lots - either 10 or 11 - see map. Parking is free for the first 75 minutes and the price of parking is reasonable at $1.50 per hour after the first 75 minutes.

11:10 am -- Santa Barbara Historical Museum

- **Price:** $7.00 (for a single adult)
- **Duration:** 45 minutes
- **Address:** 136 E De La Guerra St, Santa Barbara, CA 93101

Closed Mondays. If doing this tour on a Monday skip to the next stop or pop into the **Karpeles Manuscript Library** (free) on W. Anamapau Street.

Santa Barbara Historical Museum is a modern museum full of interesting exhibitions about Santa Barbara ranging from the Chumash period, through the times when Santa Barbara was under Spanish, then Mexican rule, and right up to the present day. The museum also has interesting rotating and temporary exhibits all year-round. Although small, the museum has several **high-tech interactive exhibits** which make things more interesting for younger visitors.

Be sure to stop at the **gift shop** on the way out if you are looking for California-themed gifts. For details on current exhibitions, times, etc. please **see website.**

11:55 am -- Walk to State Street and lunch

- **Price:** FREE
- **Duration:** 10 minutes

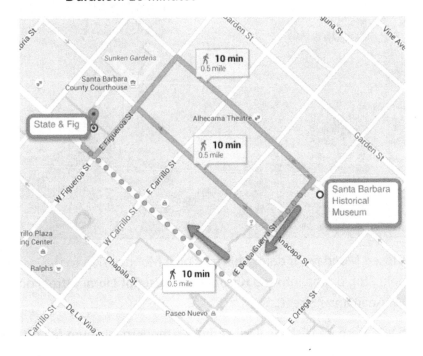

Unless you want to move your car to another parking lot, I would recommend leaving your car in the public lot and walking to the next destination. Although fairly compact, downtown Santa Barbara can be a little confusing with it's one-way streets, and sometimes it's just easier to walk.

Head south-west (left) out of the historical museum and walk down E De La Guerra Street until you reach State Street. Turn right onto State Street. Walk up State Street till you pass Figueroa. Either walk through La Arcada Plaza (you will see a building covered in ivy with an arch and walk-way into the open air plaza) till you come to State & Fig on the left, or alternatively at Figueroa Street (from State) turn right till you come to La Arcada on the left. **State & Fig** is on the right just inside the open air plaza.

12:05 pm -- Lunch: State & Fig

- **Price:** $15.00 (for a single adult)
- **Duration:** 1 hour
- **Address:** 1114 State St #18, Santa Barbara, CA 93101

State Street has a ton of options for lunch to suit every budget. **State & Fig** may be a little hard to find, but the **garlic fries, burgers, and rustic California-style decor** are worth it. Pictured is the Caprese salad. See **website** for menu.

Alternatively, check out **Benchmark Eatery** for fresh California style cuisine, **Norton's Pastrami** for "deli-cious" sandwiches, or grab a slice at **Gino's Sicilian Express**. They are all less than a 5-minute walk from State & Fig - **see map**.

1:05 pm -- Walk to Santa Barbara Museum of Art

- **Duration:** 5 minutes

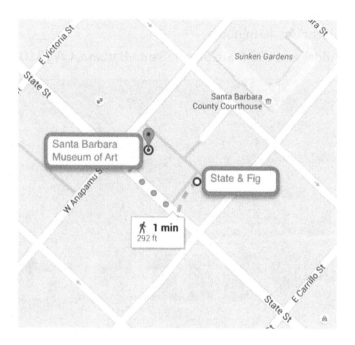

From State & Fig, the **Santa Barbara Museum of Art** is a short, 2-minute walk back via State Street.

1:10 pm -- Santa Barbara Museum of Art

- **Price:** $10.00 (for a single adult)
- **Duration:** 40 minutes
- **Address:** 1130 State Street, Santa Barbara, CA 93101

The museum is **closed Mondays**. If doing this tour on a Monday skip to the next location.

Originally housing the post office, the **Santa Barbara Museum of Art** opened in 1941 and is now the permanent home to 27,000 works of art. They also regularly host temporary exhibitions from other museums around the world. In particular, it has the biggest collection of **Monet paintings** on the west coast of America. Here you can see works such as 'Villas in Bordighera' and a very fine collection of Asian art.

The museum has numerous **free guided tours included** with the price of admission - some of these tours focus on certain subjects like sculpture or collection highlights and are worth a look if you have time. Tour times are posted on the website and at the entrance of the museum.

If travelling with children, the museum has family guides that contain gallery games, sketching activities and family-friendly information on artists and the exhibitions. On the first Thursday of the month, there is 'Family 1st Thursday' where families can create special, exhibition themed art-projects with museum teachers.

Website - be sure to check for **free entrance days**, free tour details and current exhibitions.

1:55 pm -- Walk to Santa Barbara Courthouse

- **Price:** FREE
- **Duration:** 5 minutes

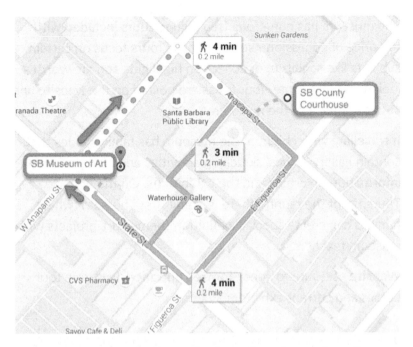

It's a short walk to the **Santa Barbara Courthouse** but allow longer if you have chosen shopping instead of visiting the Santa Barbara Museum of Art. Head northwest on State Street, turn right onto East Anapamu Street and then turn right onto Anacapa Street. You will see the courthouse on your left. Enter through the arch to the door on the right/ Follow the signposted directions to the Mural Room.

2:00 pm -- Santa Barbara Courthouse

- **Price:** FREE
- **Duration:** 1 hour
- **Address:** 1100 Anacapa Street, Santa Barbara, CA 93101

Considered to be one of the most beautiful government buildings in America, the **Santa Barbara Courthouse** was designed by William Mooser III in the Spanish-Moorish style. It was completed in 1929, just a few years after the 1925 earthquake had ruined most of the city. Today it still serves as a working courthouse with numerous weddings being held in the sunken garden (where the original courthouse stood in 1872).

You can either do the **free guided tour** at 10.30am and 2pm on weekdays (except Thursdays which only has a tour at 10.30am) or explore this beautiful courthouse alone – the Moorish tiles are stunning. If you opt for the latter, be sure to visit the clock tower and the mural room. Guided tours meet in the Mural Room (sign posted) and you can usually slip in and join the informal tour even if you are 5 minutes late. **See website for details**.

2:00 pm -- Walk back to State Street

- **Price:** FREE
- **Duration:** 5 minutes

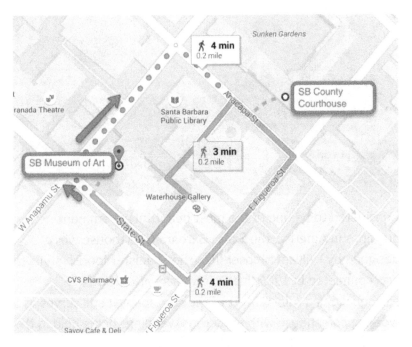

Reverse your steps to get back to **State Street.**

2:05 pm -- Shopping on State Street

- **Price:** FREE
- **Duration:** 2 hours
- **Address:** State Street, Santa Barbara, CA 93121

Because downtown Santa Barbara is so compact and walkable, it is a **shopper's paradise** with boutique and brand name stores side by side. If you are searching for unique jewelry or clothing for a friend or yourself, you will find it on State Street. The bulk of the shopping area is on **State Street** between Anapamu Street and Cota Street.

If you don't like shopping, look for a good read at **The Book Den** or just sit back, relax and people-watch with a coffee at **The French Press**. If you didn't pick this option earlier, you could also pop into the **Karpeles Manuscript Library (free)** on W. Anamapau Street.

4:05 pm -- Dinner and Drinks

- **Price:** $40.00 (for a single adult)
- **Duration:** 5 hours and 55 minutes
- **Address:** State Street, Santa Barbara, CA 93121

Photo from Louie's California Bistro Facebook page.

Santa Barbara is a **foodie's paradise** with new and exciting restaurants popping up all the time. For the latest hot spot, I recommend doing a quick google search or checking out sites like **Yelp** and **Zagat**. Otherwise, some recommendations for every budget are as follows:

La Super-Rica Taqueria. Address: 622 N. Milpas St. Price: $ Website: https://www.yelp.com/biz/la-super-rica-taqueria-santa-barbara
What they're known for: Julia Child put this hole in the wall

Mexican restaurant on the map. Expect a queue, but you never know when you might see Katy Perry (Santa Barbara's home girl) in line – she's a fan, she even mentions the restaurant in this **song**. People recommend menu item #12 or #16.

Chuck's Waterfront Grill. Address: 113 Harbor Way #180
Price: $$ Website: http://www.chuckswaterfrontgrill.com
What they're known for: You're in Santa Barbara, of course, you want to sit outside and eat. Serving up seafood classics like clam chowder as you sit watching boats in the marina sounds like a pretty good way to spend dinner. Reservations are recommended.

Louie's California Bistro. Address: The Upham, 1404 De La Vina Street. Price: $$ Website:
http://www.chuckswaterfrontgrill.com
What they're known for: Has a beautiful patio, and is in a Victorian hotel – The Upham. The food is New American, with lots of praise for the friendly staff. the shrimp and crab salad is their most popular dish. Reservations are recommended if you want to sit outside.

The Lark. Address: 131 Anacapa Street. Price: $$$ Website: http://www.thelarksb.com
What they're known for: Farm-to-table New American cuisine in a modern setting. People go wild for the Brussels sprouts here, which is saying something indeed! Reservations are recommended.

Belmond El Encanto. Address: 800 Alvarado Place. Price: $$$$
Website: http://www.belmond.com/el-encanto-santa-barbara/santa-barbara-restaurants
What they're known for: If you are looking for somewhere romantic and expensive, Belmond El Encanto has you covered.

High atop a hill with stunning panoramic views of Santa Barbara, this is five-star dining with a hefty price tag to match. Alternatively come here for breakfast or drinks for a more affordable visit. Reservations are recommended.

After Dinner Drinks and Evening Activities:

Despite being a university town, Santa Barbara doesn't have a reputation as a party town. Some visitors complain about the lack of things to do in the evenings, but there's actually lots to do if you know where to go!

There's no shortage of good bars in this town but some of the favorites include:

Whiskey Richards. Address: 437 State Street. Price: $ Website: http://www.whiskeyrichards.com
What they're known for: Stiff drinks that won't bust your budget. Pool table and bands.

Tiburon Tavern. Address: 3116 State Street. Price: $ Website: **https://www.facebook.com/tibtav**
What they're known for: Karaoke dive bar serving stiff drinks.

The Pickle Room. Address: 126 E Canon Perdido Price: $$ Website: https://www.yelp.com/biz/the-pickle-room-santa-barbara
What they're known for: Martinis with a side of egg rolls in this dark and cozy neighborhood bar.

The Good Lion. Address: 30 W Anapamu Street. Price: $$ Website: http://www.goodlioncocktails.com
What they're known for: Handcrafted cocktails like the 'Hemingway Daiquiri' and the 'Whiskey Sour'. Classy but not pretentious.

BoHenry's Cocktail Lounge. Address: 30 W Anapamu Street.
Price: $$ Website: http://www.bohenrys.com
What they're known for: Santa Barbara's own Cheers. Friendly
local bar with karaoke, pool and a good jukebox.

Milk & Honey Tapas. Address: 30 W Anapamu Street. Price: $$
Website: http://milknhoneytapas.com
What they're known for: Great service, tapas, and Mojitos.

Evening Activities:

Billiards and sushi may seem like an odd combination, but
Tuesday nights at **Q's Billiard Club and Sushi-a-go-go** is a very
popular 80s night. See website: https://www.yelp.com/biz/qs-
billiard-club-and-sushi-a-go-go-santa-barbara

If live music is your jam then head to **Velvet Jones**, a no-frills
live music venue on State Street. For calendar and tickets see
website: http://www.velvet-jones.com/

For a slightly older crowd, **SoHo** is a live music venue with
artists ranging in genre from jazz, funk, to reggae and blues. For
calendar and tickets see website: http://www.sohosb.com/.

West Wind Santa Barbara Drive-In – Just slightly north of
Santa Barbara in Goleta, you can experience the all-American
classic – the drive-in. For showtimes and tickets see website:
http://www.westwinddi.com/

Santa Barbara Bowl – The 4,500 seat amphitheatre is a great
way to catch a concert outdoors with major acts performing
often. For tickets and concert details see website:
https://sbbowl.com/

Zodo's in Goleta is a bowling alley / arcade combo with glow bowling (DJs, fog, glow in the dark balls, etc.) on Wednesday, Friday and Saturday nights. For details see website http://www.zodos.com/

Throughout the summer, the city hosts **free concerts** on Thursdays at 'Chase Palm Park'. For details see website: http://www.santabarbaraca.gov/gov/depts/parksrec/recreation/events/parkrec/concerts.asp

The city also shows **free movies** in the sunken garden of the courthouse on Fridays and at UCSB on Wednesdays. For details see website: http://www.sbparkfoundation.org/events/.

La Cumbre Plaza holds jazz concerts and food trucks throughout the summer and into fall. See website: http://www.shoplacumbre.com/events

The area is no stranger to the performing arts. It has three historic theaters: **The Arlingon theatre** shows everything from ballet to rock acts, **The Granada theatre** showcases music, movies and comedians, and **The Lobero Theatre** focuses mostly on music, and jazz in particular.

Just fancy dessert and an early end to the night? Head to **McConnells** for a scoop or two of their famously delicious ice cream which started right here in Santa Barbara in 1949. Website: http://www.mcconnells.com/

Day 2

=============

9:00 am -- East Beach Cafe

- **Price:** $10.00 (for a single adult)
- **Duration:** 1 hour
- **Address:** 1118 E Cabrillo Blvd, Santa Barbara, CA 93103

Picture from East Beach Cafe

A great way to start your stay in Santa Barbara is to enjoy breakfast on the beach. **The East Beach Cafe** is the closest you will get to actually eating on the beach without getting sand in your breakfast burrito. A firm favorite with locals, the East Beach Cafe has been serving up breakfast and lunch for good value for longer than anyone can remember. This no-frills café works very simply – stand in line, order and pay, then sit at the tables along the beach and wait for them to bring you your breakfast burrito or blueberry wheat germ pancakes to enjoy in the sun.

If you have had breakfast at your hotel, you can either skip to the next stop or take a leisure post-breakfast walk along the beach front towards the pier – **Sterns Wharf**.

Today's activities focus on two of Santa Barbara's best offerings – wine and the great outdoors. I suggest you leave your car at your hotel and either take the **electric shuttle** for 50 cents (exact change) or a car sharing service like Uber/Lyft.

10:00 am -- Santa Barbara Harbor and Shoreline Park Walk

- **Price:** FREE
- **Duration:** 2 hours
- **Address:** 1118 E Cabrillo Blvd, Santa Barbara, CA 93103

After breakfast take a nice but very pleasant easy 3-mile walk along the ocean path past the pier and harbor from East Beach Grill towards **Shoreline Park**.

Alternatively, **if you have a dog with you**, drive to **Douglas Family Preserve** for a dog-friendly (off leash) 1.5-mile walk.

If walking is not your thing, a 'duck' land and sea adventure is a fun way to get a great overview of the city. For schedule and tickets see website: http://www.out2seesb.com/

Children and animal lovers may prefer to head to Santa Barbara Zoo to feed a giraffe and see a rare California Condor – the Gibbon enclosure, in particular, is fantastic. For times, ticket details, etc. see website: http://www.sbzoo.org/ (If you are extending your stay, the zoo is a great addition for another day.)

For the more active, Santa Barbara is an ideal spot to enjoy a morning on the ocean in either a **rented stand-up paddleboard or kayak.**

12:00 pm -- Lunch

- **Price:** $10.00 (for a single adult)
- **Duration:** 1 hour
- **Address:** Anacapa St, Santa Barbara

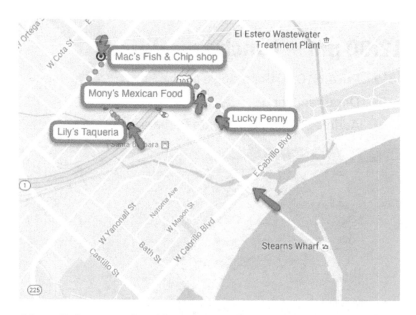

After all that exercise, I imagine you're probably starving. There are plenty of great options near Stern's Wharf, which you should head back to for our next stop after lunch.

Some lunch favorites are:

Mony's Mexican. Address: 217 E Anacapa St, Santa Barbara Price: $ Website: **https://www.yelp.com/biz/monys-mexican-food-santa-barbara**
What they're known for: People love their different salsas - pistachio, peanut butter, etc.

Lucky Penny. Address: 127 Anacapa St, Santa Barbara Price: $$ Website: **http://www.luckypennysb.com**
What they're known for: Wood-fired pizza, especially the 'Dan Russo' made with sausage, fennel, and arugula.

Lily's Taqueria. Address: 310 Chapala St, Santa Barbara Price: $
Website: **https://www.yelp.com/biz/lillys-tacos-santa-barbara-2**
What they're known for: Don't be put off by the line, it moves
fast and it's definitely worth the "weight" for delicious
authentic tacos.

1:00 pm -- Walk to Funk Zone

- **Duration:** 15 minutes

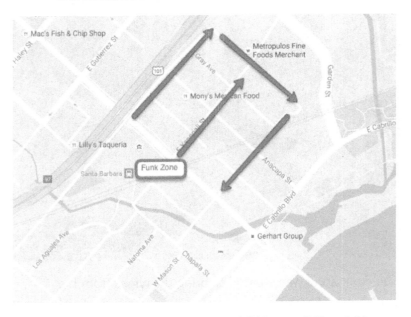

The Funk Zone is off State Street and E Yanonali Street. You
can wander up any of the streets and you will come to the main
bulk of the tasting rooms.

1:15 pm -- Funk Zone

- **Price:** $30.00 (for a single adult)
- **Duration:** 3 hours
- **Address:** State Street and E Yanonali Street, Santa Barbara

The Funk Zone was created to bring the wines from the vineyards of Santa Barbara county into the city. Not to be outdone, there are several craft beer breweries among the 20 or so wine tasting rooms like Figueroa Mountain and Brass Bear. While the area has been somewhat 'hipsterfied' all ages (as long as they are over 21) can enjoy the Funk Zone.

The choice of tasting rooms may sound overwhelming, so here are some recommendations: Head to **Kunin Wines** (pictured above) for a chilled, So Cal experience. This small, clean and bright tasting room is one of the most chilled stops. If you are looking for something edgier filled with retro items, then **Municipal Winemakers** is a good stop. Serious about your 'vino'? **Les Marchands** is the refinery you are looking for.

You can **enjoy tastings** in most of the wineries without an appointment (although if you are a large group you should make reservations). Tasting prices range from $5 - $15 dollars for tastes of between four and eight wines. It's a great opportunity to taste some of the amazing wines that have put California on the wine map. For details of events and new tasting rooms **see website**.

For a map and list of events (usually arts based) happening, see the Funk Zone **website** or see **this site for a map** of the entire urban Santa Barbara wine scene. You can also download the free **Urban Wine Trail app**.

While in the Funk Zone you may enjoy exploring the vintage shop **The Blue Door** or pop into the free **Santa Barbara Surf Museum** (it's tiny but fun!). Numerous art galleries are also popping up in the Funk Zone and make a nice in-between-stop when visiting the tasting rooms. Just don't blame me for any 'impulse' purchases!

For the **under 21** and for those who don't care for wine, how about a delicious cup of tea? If it's Friday or Saturday head to the **Four Seasons Biltmore**, otherwise check out **Anderson's Danish Bakery & Restaurant** for a Danish flair on high tea, or make a reservation (24 hrs. in advance) and enjoy the view from the terrace at **Belmond El Encanto's high tea** which is surprisingly well priced as far as high tea goes.

4:15 pm -- Dinner and Drinks

- **Price:** $40.00 (for a single adult)
- **Duration:** 5 hours and 45 minutes
- **Address:** State Street, Santa Barbara

For dinner (and you really should eat after all that wine) why not try some of the previous lunch suggestions, which also serve dinner and are situated near or in The Funk Zone. See the previous list for specific restaurants.

If none of these suit your tastes, why not try one of the dinner suggestions from day 1 that you didn't get to try? Find them all under "dinner and drinks" for day 1

Things You Need to Know

Santa Barbara, America's Riviera is a little slice of paradise with it's year-round good weather. There's plenty to see and do, from world-famous art to boutique shopping, alfresco dining, sipping on award-winning wines and beers, just lounging on the beach, or visiting a first class zoo. Santa Barbara has something for everyone.

Days of this tour can be swapped around easily, depending on your personal preference however, please note, some activities are only open certain days so check before deciding. I have also provided some suggestions for activities if you want to extend your Santa Barbara stay, under Other Activities/Events. The tour is mostly walkable and you could use public transport or ride sharing sites as Santa Barbara is a fairly compact city, unlike Los Angeles. You can also ride the **electric shuttle** for 50 cents (exact change) that loops State Street every 15 minutes or use a car-sharing service like Uber/Lyft.

Getting There From Los Angeles

Takes just over 2 hours from central Los Angeles (depending on traffic of course). The roads are well looked after and it's a fairly easy drive. Weekend (Friday and Sunday nights) traffic can be worse depending on events in the areas. There are several routes from central Los Angeles so check traffic before you leave! **Link to map route**.

You can also **take the train** from Los Angeles's Union Station to Santa Barbara then use taxis or car services like Lyft or Uber once you are there. You can also take a **Greyhound bus** from Downtown Los Angeles or the **Santa Barbara Airbus** from LAX airport.

Places to Stay

Santa Barbara has accommodation to suit pretty much everyone, though it can get expensive in high season (Mid May - August), or during special events. However, it enjoys year-round good weather with cooler temperatures from November through to March so you could plan your visit out of season. Some suggested places to stay include:

Budget: **Castillo Inn at The Beach**, **Agave Inn** or **Oasis Inn and Suites**, or **The Presido** or **The Holiday Inn Express** (great location)

Camping or RVing: This part of the coast has some **spectacular sites** but you will be a little out of the city and reservations should be made far in advance.

Mid-range hotels: **Harbor House Inn**, **Bath Street Inn**, **Hotel Santa Barbara** and **The Lemon Tree Inn**.

Luxury hotels: **Canary**, **Spanish Garden Inn** or **Simpson House Inn** or **The Upham**.

Vacation Rentals/Self Catering: **Airbnb** or **HomeAway** has a wide selection of home rentals and apartment sharing. Get an Airbnb coupon towards your first stay signing up via **this link**.

As well as the usual booking hotel websites, it is worth checking out sites like **Groupon**, **LivingSocial**, and **Goldstar** as often they have deals on hotels.

Other Useful Information

Cars: Some tips for driving: You can turn **right on a red light** unless there are signs to the contrary. When at a major intersection, after the traffic lights change, be sure to wait a few seconds as cars often skip through. In Southern California, freeways or motorways are referred as "THE 405" or "THE 1-10", and when there is a hyphen it will be referred to as "The One-Ten". Several car sharing programs are now available in Los Angeles, like **Zipcar**, **Relay Rides**, **Getaround**, or **Justshareit** etc, which can make a cheaper alternative to a rental car. Although these services are available in Los Angeles, double-check that they will allow you to take the car out of the city, and all the way to Santa Barbara. Some more tips for the first time driving in the US can be found **here**.

Parking: Parking in Santa Barbara is fairly easy, with plenty of cheap/free public parking. You can see a list of the lots on the **website** which includes real time availability. It's recommended you carry cash (a roll of quarters can be exchanged for cash at any bank), or a credit/debit card for metered parking. A list of parking sites and prices can be found **online here**. I highly recommend downloading the **Parkopedia** website/app, or the **Parkme** website/app for your smartphone.

Taxis: Either get your hotel to call you one or book online. Also, smartphone-based ride sharing services like **Lyft**, **Uber**, and **Sidecar** are popular in Santa Barbara because its downtown area is so compact. If you are using any of these services for the first time, use these discount coupon codes:

- For a Sidecar use coupon code: CLARE35
- For a Uber coupon use: UBERSELFGUIDETOLA

- For a Lyft coupon use: CLARE758131

Downtown Waterfront Shuttle: This electric tram does a loop of downtown Santa Barbara every 15 minutes and costs just 50 cents. Make sure you have the exact change. See **website** for details of route and schedule.

Pets: Santa Barbara is very dog friendly with many **dog accessible beaches**, resturants, and **hotels**.

Kids: With the exception of the Funk Zone, every stop on this two-day tour is kid-friendly. See other activities and events for more kid-friendly things to do.

Other Activities/Events

Santa Barbara has lots of events going on throughout the year, so double-check at http://santabarbaraca.com/events/ if there is something you want to see (or avoid). Some of the major events are:

- Santa Barbara Film Festival
- The Santa Barbara Arts and Crafts Show
- The Original Earth Day
- Summer Solstice Celebration
- Music Academy of the West
- California Wine Festival
- Old Spanish Days Fiesta
- California Lemon Festival
- Harbor and Seafood Festival
- Santa Barbara's annual Parade of Lights

If you want to extend your trip, Santa Barbara and the greater surrounding area have lots of other activities to enjoy. You may need a car to get to some of these suggestions from downtown Santa Barbara and those marked with a star are family friendly:

- Feed a giraffe at **Santa Barbara Zoo** *
- Tour the amazing gardens of **Lotusland** *
- Have dinner in an original stagecoach stop **Cold Spring Tavern***
- Wine tasting in the picturesque **Los Olivos**
- Taste the world famous Pea soup at **Andersen's** in Bullerton *
- See swarms of migrating Monarchs at **Goleta Butterfly Farm** *

- Tour the historic and well preserved **Casa Del Herrero***
- Take a boat tour **Whale watching** *
- Visit the Danish town of **Solvang** *
- Pet miniature donkeys at **Seein' Spots Farm** *
- Smell the amazing **Lavender farm** in Los Olivos *
- **Santa Barbara Natural History Museum** and Sea Center (consider an **SB Nature Pass**) *
- **Santa Barbara Maritime Museum** *
- Tour the beautiful coastline with **Santa Barbara's Li' Toot water taxi** *
- Take a tour of the historic **Stow House** in Goelta*
- Visit the **Sadako Peace Garden**
- Hike to Knapp's Castle *
- Hike to **Chumash Painted Cave State Historic Park** *

Useful Websites:

- Official tourism website: **http://santabarbaraca.com**
- Santa Barbara magazine: **http://sbmag.com**
- Car Free Santa Barbara: **http://www.santabarbaracarfree.org**
- Downtown Santa Barbara: **http://www.downtownsb.org**
- Santa Barbara lifestyle magazine: **http://www.santabarbaralifeandstyle.com**

About the Author

Clare Auchterlonie

Since 2001 I have lived in Los Angeles, I came here on a whim from London and for the most part I haven't looked back. Maybe once, when I ran out of tea bags. Always looking for new things to discover in my adopted city – I'm a Resident Tourist!

FEEDBACK AND MORE INFORMATION:

If you have questions or feedback on this tour please feel free to contact me at **restouristLA@gmail.com**

You can also follow me on Twitter @ResTourist or Instagram @ResidentTouristLA or Facebook **https://www.facebook.com/selfguidetoLA**

See the rest of my Southern California tours available on Amazon: http://tinyurl.com/LAselfguide or through Unanchor: **http://www.unanchor.com/user/clareauchterlonie**

Unanchor

Chief Itinerary Coordinator

Unanchor wants your opinion!

Your next travel adventure starts now. A simple review on Amazon will grant you and a travel buddy, friend, or human of your choosing any of the wonderful Unanchor digital itineraries for free.

What a deal!

Leave a Review

- Leave a review: http://www.amazon.com/unanchor

Collect your guides

- Send an email to reviews@unanchor.com with a link to your review.
- Wait with bated breath.
- Receive your new travel adventure in your inbox!

Other Unanchor Itineraries

Africa

- One Day in Africa - A Guide to Tangier
- Cape Town - What not to miss on a 4-day first-timers' itinerary
- Johannesburg/Pretoria: A 4-Day South Africa Tour Itinerary

Asia

- 4 Days in Bishkek On a Budget
- Beijing Must Sees, Must Dos, Must Eats - 3-Day Tour Itinerary
- 2 Days in Shanghai: A Budget-Conscious Peek at Modern China
- A 3-Day Tryst with 300-Year-Old Kolkata
- Kolkata (Calcutta): 2 Days of Highlights
- 3-Day Budget Delhi Itinerary
- Delhi in 3 Days - A Journey Through Time
- 3 Days Highlights of Mumbai
- Nozawa Onsen's Winter Secrets - A 3-Day Tour
- 3-Day Highlights of Tokyo
- Tour Narita During an Airport Layover
- 3 Days in the Vibrant City of Seoul and the Serene Countryside of Gapyeong
- A First Timer's Weekend Guide to Ulaanbaatar
- The Very Best of Moscow in 3 Days
- Saint Petersburg in Three Days

Central America and the Caribbean

- Old San Juan, Puerto Rico 2-Day Walking Itinerary
- Two Exciting Days in Dutch Sint Maarten - Hello Cruisers!
- Two Amazing Days in St. Croix, USVI - Hello Cruisers!

Europe

- Beginner's Iceland - A four-day self-drive itinerary
- Mostar - A City with Soul in 1 Day
- 3 Days in Brussels - The grand sites via the path less trodden
- Zagreb For Art Lovers: A Three-Day Itinerary
- 3-Day Prague Beer Pilgrimage
- Best of Prague - 3-Day Itinerary
- 3 Days in Copenhagen - Explore Like a Local
- Best of Copenhagen 2-Day Walking Itinerary
- Christmas in Copenhagen - A 2-Day Guide
- 3 Days in Helsinki
- Highlights of Budapest in 3 Days
- 3 Days in Dublin City - City Highlights, While Eating & Drinking Like a Local
- Weekend Break: Tbilisi - Crown Jewel of the Caucasus
- 2 Days In Berlin On A Budget
- A 3-Day Guide to Berlin, Germany
- 3 Days of Fresh Air in Moldova's Countryside
- Amsterdam 3-Day Alternative Tour: Not just the Red Light District
- Amsterdam Made Easy: A 3-Day Guide
- Two-day tour of Utrecht: the smaller, less touristy Amsterdam!
- Krakow: Three-Day Tour of Poland's Cultural Capital
- Best of Warsaw 2-Day Itinerary
- Lisbon in 3 Days: Budget Itinerary
- Braşov - Feel the Pulse of Transylvania in 3 Days
- Lausanne 1-Day Tour Itinerary
- Belgrade: 7 Days of History on Foot

France

- Paris to Chartres Cathedral: 1-Day Tour Itinerary
- A 3-Day Tour of Mont St Michel, Normandy and Brittany
- Art Lovers' Paris: A 2-Day Artistic Tour of the City of Lights
- Paris 1-Day Itinerary - Streets of Montmartre
- Paris 3-Day Walking Tour: See Paris Like a Local
- Paris 4-Day Winter Wonderland
- Paris for Free: 3 Days
- The Best of Paris in One Day

Greece
- Athens 3-Day Highlights Tour Itinerary
- Chania & Sfakia, Greece & Great Day Trips Nearby (5-Day Itinerary)
- Santorini, Greece in 3 Days: Living like a Local
- 2-Day Beach Tour: Travel like a Local in Sithonia Peninsula, Halkidiki, Greece
- Day Trip From Thessaloniki to Kassandra Peninsula, Halkidiki, Greece
- Thessaloniki, Greece - 3-Day Highlights Itinerary

Italy

- A Day on Lake Como, Italy
- 3-Day Florence Walking Tours
- Florence, Italy 3-Day Art & Culture Itinerary
- Milan Unknown - A 3-day tour itinerary
- 3 Days of Roman Adventure: spending time and money efficiently in Rome
- A 3-Day Tour Around Ancient Rome
- Discover Rome's Layers: A 3-Day Walking Tour
- See Siena in a Day
- Landscape, Food, & Trulli: 1 Week in Puglia, the Valle d'Itria, and Matera
- Three Romantic Walks in Venice

Spain

- 3-Day Highlights of Barcelona Itinerary
- FC Barcelona: More than a Club (A 1-Day Experience)
- Ibiza on a Budget - Three-Day Itinerary
- Three days exploring Logroño and La Rioja by public transport
- Málaga, Spain – 2-Day Tour from the Moors to Picasso
- Mijas - One Day Tour of an Andalucían White Village
- Two-Day Tour in Sunny Seville, Spain
- Best of Valencia 2-Day Guide

United Kingdom

- Bath: An Exploring Guide - 2-Day Itinerary
- History, Culture, and Craic: 3 Days in Belfast, Ireland
- 2-Day Brighton Best-of Walks & Activities
- Bristol in 2 Days: A Local's Guide
- Two-Day Self-Guided Walks - Cardiff

- The Best of Edinburgh: A 3-Day Journey from Tourist to Local
- 3-Day London Tour for Olympic Visitors
- An Insider's Guide to the Best of London in 3 Days
- Done London? A 3-day itinerary for off the beaten track North Norfolk
- London 1-Day Literary Highlights
- London for Free :: Three-Day Tour
- London's Historic City Wall Walk (1-2 days)
- London's South Bank - Off the Beaten Track 1-Day Tour
- London's Villages - A 3-day itinerary exploring Hampstead, Marylebone and Notting Hill
- Low-Cost, Luxury London - 3-Day Itinerary
- The 007 James Bond Day Tour of London
- MADchester - A Local's 3-Day Guide To Manchester
- One Day in Margate, UK on a Budget

Middle East

- Paphos 3-Day Itinerary: Live like a local!
- Adventure Around Amman: A 2-Day Itinerary
- Amman 2-Day Cultural Tour
- Doha 2-Day Stopover Cultural Tour
- Doha Surf and Turf: A two-day itinerary
- 3 Days as an Istanbulite: An Istanbul Itinerary
- Between the East and the West, a 3-Day Istanbul Itinerary

North America

Canada

- Relax in Halifax for Two Days Like a Local
- An Insider's Guide to Toronto: Explore the City Less Traveled in Three Days
- The Best of Toronto - 2-Day Itinerary
- Toronto: A Multicultural Retreat (3-day itinerary)

Mexico

- Cancun and Mayan Riviera 5-Day Itinerary (3rd Edition)
- Everything to see or do in Mexico City - 7-Day Itinerary
- Mexico City 3-Day Highlights Itinerary
- Todo lo que hay que ver o hacer en la Ciudad de México - Itinerario de 7 Días
- Your Chiapas Adventure: San Cristobal de las Casas and Palenque, Mexico 5-Day Itinerary

United States

East Coast

- Girls' 3-Day Weekend Summer Getaway in Asheville, NC
- Atlanta 3-Day Highlights
- Baltimore: A Harbor, Parks, History, Seafood & Art - 3-Day Itinerary
- Boston 2-Day Historic Highlights Itinerary
- Navigating Centuries of Boston's Nautical History in One Day
- Rainy Day Boston One-Day Itinerary
- Brooklyn, NY 2-Day Foodie Tour
- The Weekenders Guide To Burlington, Vermont
- A Local's Guide to the Hamptons 3 Day Itinerary
- Weekend Day Trip from New York City: The Wine & Whiskey Trail
- 2 Days Exploring Haunted Key West
- 3 Day PA Dutch Country Highlights (Lancaster County, PA)
- Day Trek Along the Hudson River
- A Local's Guide to Montauk, New York in 2 Days - From the Ocean to the Hills
- New Haven Highlights: Art, Culture & History 3-Day Itinerary
- Day Trip from New York City: Mountains, Falls, & a Funky Town
- 3-Day Amazing Asian Food Tour of New York City!
- Hidden Bars of New York City's East Village & Lower East Side: A 2-Evening Itinerary
- Jewish New York in Two Days
- Lower Key, Lower Cost: Lower Manhattan - 1-Day Itinerary
- New York City - First Timer's 2-Day Walking Tour
- New York City's Lower East Side, 1-Day Tour Itinerary
- New York Like A Native: Five Boroughs in Six Days
- 3-Day Discover Orlando Itinerary

- Five Days in the Wild Outer Banks of North Carolina
- Two Days in Philadelphia
- Pittsburgh: Three Days Off the Beaten Path
- Day Trip from New York City: Heights of the Hudson Valley (Bridges and Ridges)
- RVA Haunts, History, and Hospitality: Three Days in Richmond, Virginia
- Savannah 3-Day Highlights Itinerary
- Three Days in the Sunshine City of St. Petersburg, Florida
- Washington, DC in 4 Days
- Washington, DC: 3 Days Like a Local

Central US

- A Laid-Back Long Weekend in Austin, TX
- 3-Day Chicago Highlights Itinerary
- 6-Hour "Layover" Chicago
- Chicago Food, Art and Funky Neighborhoods in 3 Days
- Famous Art & Outstanding Restaurants in Chicago 1-Day Itinerary
- Family Weekend in Columbus, OH
- Ohio State Game Day Weekend
- Corpus Christi: The Insider Guide for a 4-Day Tour
- The Best of Kansas City: 3-Day Itinerary
- La Grange, Kentucky: A 3-Day Tour Itinerary
- Louisville: Three Days in Derby City
- New Orleans 3-Day Itinerary
- Paris Foodie Classics: 1 Day of French Food
- Wichita From Cowtown to Air Capital in 2 Days

West Coast

- Orange County 3-Day Budget Itinerary
- Cruisin' Asbury like a Local in 1 Day
- A Day on Bainbridge Island
- Beverly Hills, Los Angeles - 1-Day Tour
- Beer Lovers 3-Day Guide To Northern California
- The Best of Boulder, CO: A Three-Day Guide
- Lesser-known Oahu in 4 Days on a Budget
- Local's Guide to Oahu - 3-Day Tour Itinerary
- Summer in Jackson Hole: Local Tips for the Perfect Three to Five Day Adventure
- Tackling 10 Must-Dos on the Big Island in 3 Days
- Las Vegas - Gaming Destination Diversions - Ultimate 3-Day Itinerary

- Las Vegas on a Budget - 3-Day Itinerary
- 2-Day Los Angeles Vegan and Vegetarian Foodie Itinerary
- Downtown Los Angeles 1-Day Walking Tour
- Hollywood, Los Angeles - 1-Day Walking Tour
- Los Angeles 4-Day Itinerary (partly using Red Tour Bus)
- Los Angeles Highlights 3-Day Itinerary
- Los Angeles On A Budget - 4-Day Tour Itinerary
- Sunset Strip, Los Angeles - 1-Day Walking Tour
- An Active 2-3 Days In Moab, Utah
- Beyond the Vine: 2-Day Napa Tour
- Wine, Food, and Fun: 3 Days in Napa Valley
- Palm Springs, Joshua Tree & Salton Sea: A 3-Day Itinerary
- Portland Bike and Bite: A 2-Day Itinerary
- Three Days Livin' as a True and Local Portlander
- Weekend Tour of Portland's Craft Breweries, Wineries, & Distilleries
- Best of the Best: Three-Day San Diego Itinerary
- San Francisco 2-Day Highlights Itinerary
- San Francisco Foodie Weekend Itinerary
- The Tech Lover's 48-Hour Travel Guide to Silicon Valley & San Francisco
- Alaska Starts Here - 3 Days in Seward
- Three Days in Central California's Wine Country
- Tucson: 3 Days at the Intersection of Mexico, Native America & the Old West

Oceania

- The Blue Mountains: A weekend of nature, culture and history.
- A Weekend Snapshot of Melbourne
- An Afternoon & Evening in Melbourne's Best Hidden Bars
- Laneway Melbourne: A One-Day Walking Tour
- Magic of Melbourne 3-Day Tour
- Two Wheels and Pair of Cozzies: the Best of Newcastle in 3 Days
- Best of Perth's Most Beautiful Sights in 3 Days
- A Weekend Snapshot of Sydney
- Sydney, Australia - 3-Day **Best Of** Itinerary
- Enjoy the Rebuild - Christchurch 2-Day Tour
- The Best of Wellington: 3-Day Itinerary

South America

- An Insider's Guide to the Best of Buenos Aires in 3 Days
- Buenos Aires Best Kept Secrets: 2-Day Itinerary
- Sights & Sounds of São Paulo - 3-Day Itinerary
- Cuenca, Ecuador - A 3-Day Discovery Tour
- A 1-Day Foodie's Dream Tour of Arequipa
- Arequipa - A 2-Day Itinerary for First-Time Visitors
- Cusco and the Sacred Valley - a five-day itinerary for a first-time visitor
- Little Known Lima 3-Day Tour

Southeast Asia

- Between the Skyscrapers - Hong Kong 3-Day Discovery Tour
- Art and Culture in Ubud, Bali – 1-Day Highlights
- Go with the Sun to Borobudur & Prambanan in 1 Day
- A 3-Day Thrilla in Manila then Flee to the Sea
- Manila on a Budget: 2-Day Itinerary
- A First Timer's Guide to 3 Days in the City that Barely Sleeps - Singapore
- Family Friendly Singapore - 3 Days in the Lion City
- Singapore: 3 Fun-Filled Days on this Tiny Island
- The Affordable Side of Singapore: A 4-Day Itinerary
- The Two Worlds of Kaohsiung in 5 Days
- 72 Hours in Taipei: The All-rounder
- Girls' Weekend in Bangkok: Shop, Spa, Savour, Swoon
- The Ins and Outs of Bangkok: A 3-Day Guide
- *Saigon 3-Day Beyond the Guidebook Itinerary*

Unanchor is a global family for travellers to experience the world with the heart of a local.

UNANCHOR

Made in United States
North Haven, CT
25 February 2022

16499283R00036